MORE

CHINESE SLANGUAGE

A *FUN* VISUAL GUIDE TO MANDARIN TERMS AND PHRASES BY MIKE ELLIS

C000053122

GIBBS SMITH
TO ENRICH AND INSPIRE HUMANKIND

DEDICATED TO SUZANNE, GINNY, MIKEY & PHIDGETTE

First Edition
18 17 16 15 14   5 4 3 2

Published by
Gibbs Smith
P.O. Box 667
Layton, Utah 84041

1.800.835.4993 orders
www.gibbs-smith.com

Designed by michelvrana.com

Gibbs Smith books are printed on paper produced
from sustainable PEFC-certified forest/controlled
wood source. Learn more at www.pefc.org.
Printed and bound in Hong Kong

Library of Congress Cataloging-in-Publication Data

Ellis, Mike, 1961–
  More Chinese slanguage : a fun visual
guide to Chinese terms and phrases
/ Mike Ellis. — First Edition.
    pages cm.
  ISBN 978-1-4236-3615-1
1. Chinese language—Conversation and
phrase books—English. I. Title.
  PL1125.E6E44 2013
  495.1'83421—dc23
                          2013027901

CONTENTS

HOW TO USE THIS BOOK

If you have always wanted to learn the basics of Mandarin, but traditional methods seemed overwhelming or intimidating, this book is for you! Just follow the directions below and soon you'll be able to say dozens of words and phrases in Mandarin.

• Follow the illustrated prompts and say the phrase quickly and smoothly with equal emphasis on the words or syllables. While Mandarin is a tonal language, you'll still be understood if you speak clearly and evenly. A strikethrough means don't pronounce that letter.

• Learn to string together words or phrases to create many more phrases.

• The words and phrases are sorted alphabetically within each chapter to make finding them easier.

• Draw your own pictures to help with memorization and pronunciation.

Note: This book may produce Americanized Mandarin.

For free sound bytes, visit slanguage.com.

Congratulations
祝贺您 *Zhù hè nín*

Jew Honey

You She Oh

Excellent
优秀 *Yōu xiù*

Dewey Boo Cheap

Excuse me
对不起 *Duì bù qǐ*

Hen How

Fairly well
很好 *Hěn hǎo*

Friend
朋友 *Péng yǒu*

Pong Yo

Good evening
晚上好
Wǎn shàng hǎo

1 Shun How

Good-bye
再见 *Zài jiàn*

Sigh Jean An

I love you
我爱你 *Wǒ ài nǐ*

Woe Eye Knee

Have a good day
有一个很好的一天
*Yǒu yī gè hěn hǎo
de yī tiān*

Yo You Go Hen How

Dee Yee Tee An

Hen Joe Mayo Ken Down

Long time, no see
很久没有看到
Hěn jiǔ méi yǒu kàn dào

My name is . . .
我的名字是······
Wǒ de míng zì shì . . .

Woe Demeans Us She . . .

Nice to meet you
很高兴见到你
Hěn gāo xìng jiàn dào nǐ

Hen Gown Sheen Tee

Yen Down Knee

No kidding
不开玩笑
Bù kāi wán xiào

Boo Kite 1 Shout

Please
请 *Qǐng*

Ching

So-so
马马虎虎
Mǎ mǎ hǔ hǔ

Mama Who Who

Welcome
欢迎　*Huān yíng*

1 Ying

What a good surprise!
好惊奇!　*Hǎo jīng qí!*

How Ching Cheap!

With pleasure
高兴　*Gāo xīng*

Gouging

Are you crazy?
你疯了吗？
Nǐ fēng le ma?

Knee Fun Glum Ma?

Can you tell me . . . ?
可不可以告诉我······？
Kě bù kě yǐ gào su wǒ . . . ?

Kabuki Gown Sew . . . ?

Do you speak English?
你会说英语吗？
Nǐ huì shuō yīng yǔ ma?

Knee Way Shoe

Ying You Ma?

How long?
多久? *Duō jiǔ?*

Due Joe?

How many?
多少? *Duō shǎo?*

Due Shout?

How much does it cost?
多少钱?
Duō shǎo qián?

Due Shout Yen?

How old are you?
你多大年龄?
Nǐ duō dà nián líng?

Knee Due Don Yen Ling?

How's it going?
近况如何?
Jìn kuàng rú hé?

Gin Kwan Rue Huh

Is that good?
好了吗?　*Hǎo le ma?*

Ha Lay Ma?

What did you say?
你说什么?
Nǐ shuō shén má?

Knee Show Shen Ma?

What's wrong?
出了什么问题?
Chū le shén má wèn tí?

Chew Lesson Ma Went He

What's your name?
您的名字叫什么?
Nín de míng zì jiào shén má?

Ninja Ming's Duh

Chow Shoe Ma

Where do you live?
你住在哪里?
Nǐ zhù zài nǎ lǐ?

Neat Chew Sign Ollie?

Which way?
哪个方向?
Nǎ ge fāng xiàng?

Naga Function?

16 QUESTIONS

To answer
回答 *Huí dá*

Way Do̶t̶ •

To attach
附上 *Fù shàng*

Foo̶l̶ Sung

To beat
打 *Dǎ*

• **Do̶t̶**

To bring
带来 *Dài lái*

Die Lie

To burn
烧　*Shāo*

Shout

To chatter
喋喋不休的谈
Dié dié bù xiū de tán

Day Day Boo Shoe

Debt Tongue

To complain
抱怨　*Bào yuàn*

Bow Yen

To cry
哭 *Kū*

Coo

To deceive
欺骗 *Qī piàn*

Cheap Pea End

To dig
挖 *Wā*

Watt

To do
做 *Zuò*

Zoo

To forbid
禁止 *Jìn zhǐ*

Jean Should

To give
给 *Gěi*

Gay

To hear
听到 *Tīng dào*

Ting Down

To hit
打 *Dǎ*

Dot

To joke
讲笑话
Jiǎng xiào huà

Chow Shout Ha

To make mistakes
犯错误　　*Fàn cuò wù*

Fang Swap Woo

To meet
遇见　　*Yù jiàn*

You Gin

To persuade
说服　　*Shuō fú*

Show Fool

To protect 保护 *Bǎo hù*	**Bout Who**
To repair 修理 *Xiū lǐ*	**Show Lee**
To reply 答覆 *Dá fù*	● **Dot Foot**
To reside 住 *Zhù*	**Zoo**

To sit
坐 *Zuò*

Zoo Ah

To speak
说 *Shuō*

Show

To speak fluently
说话流利
Shuō huà liú lì

Show What Lay Oh Lee

To spend
花费 *Huā fèi*

What Fey

To take
拿 *Ná*

Knot

Chow Ship

To try
尝试 *Cháng shì*

To unfold
打开 *Dǎ kāi*

● Dot Kite

ADJECTIVES AND ADVERBS

Again
再 *Zài*

Sigh

Almost
几乎 *Jǐ hū*

Jean Who

At first
起初 *Qǐ chū*

Cheap Chew

Dot

Big
大 *Dà*

Confident
有信心　*Yǒu xìn xīn*

Yo Sheen Sheen

Crazy
疯狂的
Fēng kuáng de

Funk Wanda

Empty
空的　*Kōng de*

Con Duh

Even if
即使　*Jí shǐ*

Jean She

Familiar
熟悉　*Shú xī*

Shoe See

Fantastic
奇妙　*Qí miào*

Cheap Meow

Free
免费　*Miǎn fèi*

Me An Fay

Funny
滑稽　*Huá jī*

What Jean

Horrible
可怕　*Kě pà*

Cup Pa

Instead of . . .
而不······
Ér bù shì . . .

Are Boo Ship . . .

Kind
样　*Yàng*

Young

Lazy
怠惰的　*Dài duò de*

Die Do It Duh

A little bit
一点点　*Yī diǎn diǎn*

Edie And Dee An

A lot
很多　*Hěn duō*

Hen Duo

Maybe
或许　*Huò xǔ*

Hoe Shoe

Naughty
调皮　*Tiáo pí*

Tee Owl Pea

Noisy
嘈杂   *Cáo zá*

Towel Todd

Boo Gun Shin Shoe

Not interesting
不感兴趣
Bù gǎn xìng qù

Nowhere
到处都无
Dào chù dōu wú

Down Chew Doe Woo

Ordinary
普通   *Pǔ tōng*

Put Tongue

Polite
有礼貌   *Yǒu lǐ mào*

Yo Lee Ma

Pretty
漂亮   *Piào liang*

Pea Out Lee Ann

Probably
大概   *Dà gài*

Dot Guy

Rather
宁可   *Nìng kě*

Knee 'n Cup

Really
真的吗 *Zhēn de ma*

Gin Day Ma

Rich
富 *Fù*

Fool

Short
矮 *Ǎi*

Eye

Shy
害羞 *Hài xiū*

High Show

Simple 简单 *Jiǎn dān*	**Gin Don**
Small 小 *Xiǎo*	**Shout**
Tall 高大 *Gāo dà*	**Gown Dot**
There 那里 *Nà lǐ*	**Not Lee**

Together
一起 *Yī qǐ*

Each Eat

Unlucky
不幸的 *Bù xìng de*

Boo Sheen Duh

Upside down
倒挂 *Dào guà*

Down Guano

Well-behaved
很乖 *Hěn guāi*

Hung Why

FOOD AND RESTAURANTS

Do you have . . . ?
你有吗 · · · · · ?
Nǐ yǒu ma . . . ?

Knee Yo Ma . . . ?

I'd like . . .
我想 · · · · · ·
Wǒ xiǎng . . .

Woe Shower . . .

Apricot
杏 *Xìng*

Shing

Avocado
鳄梨 *È lí*

Early

Beet
甜菜 *Tián cài*

Tee Ann's Eye

Broccoli
西兰花 *Xī lán huā*

She Land What

Butter
牛油 *Niú yóu*

New Yo

Cake
蛋糕 *Dàn gāo*

Dan Gown

Chicken
鸡　*Jī*

Jean

Cocoa
可可　*Kě kě*

Cocoa

Corn
玉米　*Yù mǐ*

You Me

Cup
茶杯　*Chá bēi*

Chaw Bay

Garlic
蒜 *Suàn*

Swan

Glass
玻璃 *Bō lí*

Boo Lee

Ice cream
冰淇淋 *Bīng qí lín*

Bing She Lean

Jar
缸 *Gāng*

Gong

Knife
刀 *Dāo*

Down

Knee Mung

Lemon
柠檬 *Níng méng*

Mandarin
桔子 *Jié zi*

G.I.s

Orange
橙 *Chéng*

Chung

Peach 桃 *Táo*	**Town**
Pepper 胡椒 *Hú jiāo*	**Who Chow**
Plum 梅子 *Méi zi*	**Maids**
Pork 猪肉 *Zhū ròu*	**Jew Joe**

Potato
马铃薯   *Mǎ líng shǔ*

Ma Ling Shoe

Salad
沙拉   *Shā lā*

Shah Lot

Salt
盐   *Yán*

Yen

Spicy
辣   *Là*

Lot

Tangerine
蜜桔 *Mì jú*

Me Shoe

Taste
味道 *Wèi dào*

Way Down

Tea
茶 *Chá*

Chaw

To order
订购 *Dìng gòu*

Dean Go

To peel
脱皮   *Tuō pí*

Toe Pea

To swallow
吞   *Tūn*

Twin

Vinegar
醋   *Cù*

Swoon

Water
水   *Shuǐ*

Sway

Accounting
会计 *Kuài jì*

Why Jean

Finance
金融 *Jīn róng*

Jean Wrong

Housewife
主妇 *Zhǔ fù*

Chew Foot

Lawyer
律师 *Lǜ shī*

Louie Ship

Letter 书信 *Shū xìn*	**Sue Shin**
Management 管理 *Guǎn lǐ*	**Guano Lee**
Manager 经理 *Jīng lǐ*	**Jing Lee**
Note 笔记 *Bǐ jì*	**Bee Jean**

Nurse
护士 *Hù shì*

Who Ship

Order
订单 *Dìng dān*

Ding Don

Owner
业主 *Yè zhǔ*

Yay Jew

Painter
油漆工 *Yóu qī gōng*

Yo She Going

Pilot
飞行员 *Fēi xíng yuán*

Fay Shing Young

Problem
问题 *Wèn tí*

When Tee

Salesperson
售货员
Shòu huò yuán

Show Who Yen

Secretary
秘书 *Mì shū*

Me Shoe

Soldier
军人 *Jūn rén*

Jean Wren

To repair
修理 *Xiū lǐ*

Show Lee

Vacation
休假 *Xiū jiǎ*

Shoe Chow

Veterinarian
兽医 *Shòu yī*

Show Yee

Cash
现金 *Xiàn jīn*

Shan Jean

Cheap
便宜的 *Piàn yí de*

Pea Ann Eat Duh

Coin
硬币 *Yìng bì*

Yin Bee

Credit
信用 *Xìn yòng*

Shin Young

Department store
百货商店
Bǎi huò shāng diàn

Buy What Shun Din

Gift
礼物　*Lǐ wù*

Lee Woo

Grocery store
杂货铺　*Zá huò pù*

Zow Who Ah Pool

Jewelry
珠宝　*Zhū bǎo*

Jew Bout

Newsstand 报摊 *Bào tān*	**Bout Ton**
Shopping cart 购物车 *Gòu wù chē*	**Go Woodchuck**
Shopping mall 购物中心 *Gòu wù zhōng xīn*	**Go Woo John Sheen**
Store 店铺 *Diàn pù*	**Dee Ann Pool**

Supermarket
超级市场
Chāo jí shì cháng

Chow Jean She Chong

To make change
找零头   *Zhǎo ling tóu*

Chow Ling Toe

To make out a check
开支票   *Kai zhi piao*

Kite Zippy Out

To sell
出售   *Chū shòu*

Chew Show

Vending machine
自动售买机
Zì dòng shòu mǎi jī

Sit Dong Show My Jean

Withdrawal
银行提款
Yín háng tí kuǎn

Ying Hong Teak 1

Beret
贝雷帽 *Bèi léi mào*

Bay Lame Out

Boot
开机 *Kāi jī*

Kite Jean

Bracelet
手镯 *Shǒu zhuó*

Show Joe Uh

Button
钮 *Niǔ*

Knee You

Clothes
衣服 *Yī fú*

Yee Fool

Coat
外套 *Wài tào*

White How

Comfortable
舒服的 *Shū fú de*

Shoe Food Duh

Cotton
棉 *Mián*

Me Ann

Elegant
优雅　*Yōu yǎ*

Yo Yacht

Gloves
手套　*Shǒu tào*

Show Town

Pajamas
睡衣　*Shuì yī*

Sway Yee

Pants
裤　*Kù*

Coo

Pocket
口袋 *Kǒu dài*

Coat Die

Sandals
凉鞋 *Liáng xié*

Lee Young Shear

Socks
袜子 *Wà zi*

Wazoo

Stockings
丝袜 *Sī wà*

Sue What

Stripe
斑纹 *Bān wén*

Ban When

To match
配对 *Pèi duì*

Paid Way

To take off
脱下 *Tuō xià*

Toe Shah

Vest
背心 *Bèi xīn*

Bay Sheen

Wallet
皮夹子   *Pí jiā zi*

Peach Yacht Sue

Wristwatch
手表   *Shǒu biǎo*

Show Bee Out

Zipper
拉链   *Lā liàn*

Lolly Ann

Balcony
阳台　*Yáng tái*

Young Tie

Bathroom
浴室　*Yù shì*

You Ship

Broom
扫帚　*Sǎo zhǒu*

Sound Jowl

Clay
黏土　*Nián tǔ*

Knee End 2

Coffeemaker
咖啡壶　*Kā fēi hú*

Café Who

Convenience
便利　*Biàn lì*

Bee End Lee

Dishes
碗碟　*Wǎn dié*

1 Dee Yet

Dishwasher
洗碗机　*Xǐ wǎn jī*

She 1 Jean

Furniture
家具 *Jiā jù*

Jaw Jew

Housework
家务 *Jiā wù*

Jaw Woo

Kettle
水壶 *Shuǐ hú*

Shay Who

Lid
盖 *Gài*

Guy

Lock
锁　*Sǔo*

Sew

Oven
炉　*Lú*

Lou

Plank
板　*Bǎn*

Bun

Porch
门廊　*Mén láng*

Men Lung

Pump
唧筒 *Jī tǒng*

Scissors
剪刀 *Jiǎn dāo*

Stairs
楼梯 *Lóu tī*

Vase
花瓶 *Huā píng*

Jean Tongue

Jean End Town

Low Tee

What Ping

Washing machine
洗衣机 *Xǐ yī jī*

She Yee Jean

Window
窗口 *Chuāng kǒu*

Chunk Cow

Wood
木 *Mù*

Moo

Average 平均 *Píng jūn*	**Ping June**

Average
平均 *Píng jūn*

Ping June

A degree
度 *Dù*

Due

Height
高度 *Gāo dù*

Gown Due

Percent
百分之 *Bǎi fēn zhī*

Buy Fun Jean

A piece
片 *Piàn*

Pea Ann

Thickness
厚度 *Hòu dù*

How Due

To weigh
估量 *Gū liàng*

Ghoul Lee Young

Unit
单元 *Dān yuán*

Don You When

One
一　*Yī*

Yee

Two
二　*Èr*

Earth

Three
三　*Sān*

Sand

Four
四　*Sì*

Sun

Five
五 *Wǔ*

Woo

Six
六 *Liù*

Leo

Seven
七 *Qī*

Cheap

Eight
八 *Bā*

Baa

Nine
九 *Jiǔ*

Joe

She

Ten
十 *Shí*

Hundred
百 *Bǎi*

Buy

Thousand
千 *Qiān*

Chin

Million
百万 *Bǎi wàn*

Buy 1

Number
数 *Shù*

Sh'what

Ordinal
顺序数 *Shùn xù shù*

Sun She Sue

Airplane
飞机 *Fēi jī*

Fay Jean

Aisle
过道 *Guò dào*

Go Down

Customs
海关 *Hǎi guān*

Hike 1

Departure
出发 *Chū fā*

Chew Fog

Driver
司机 *Sī jī*

Sit Jean

Ferry
渡船 *Dù chuán*

Due Chew 1

Flight
航班 *Háng bān*

Hung Ban

Horn
喇叭 *Lǎ bā*

Lot Baa

Jet
喷气式飞机
Pēn qì shì fēi jī

Pen She Sun Fay Jean

Luggage
行李 *Xíng lǐ*

Shing Lee

Passport
护照 *Hùz hào*

Who Jowl

Platform
平台 *Píng tái*

Ping Tie

Road 道路 *Dào lù*	**Down Lou**
Speed 速度 *Sù dù*	**Sue Do**
Time zone 时区 *Shí qū*	**Ship Chew**
Street 街道 *Jiē dào*	**Jay Down**

To arrive
到达　*Dào dá*

Down Dot

To take a trip
走一趟　*Zǒu yī tàng*

Zoë Tongue

To tow
拖　*Tuō*

Toe

Tow truck
拖车　*Tuō chē*

Toe Chuck

Beige
米色 *Mǐ sè*

Me Sun

Black
黑色 *Hēi sè*

Hay Sun

Blue
蓝色 *Lán sè*

Lawn Sun

Brown
褐色 *Hè sè*

Huh Sun

A color
色　*Sè*

Sun

Gold
金色　*Jīn sè*

Gin Sun

Gray
灰色　*Huī sè*

We Sun

Green
绿色　*Lǜ sè*

Louisa

Maroon
栗色 *Lì sè*

Lisa

Orange
橙色 *Chéng sè*

Chunk Sun

Pink
粉色 *Fěn sè*

Fun Sun

Red
红色 *Hóng sè*

Hong Sun

To color
颜色 *Yán sè*

Yan Sun

Turquoise
绿松石 *Lǜ song shí*

Lou Song She

White
白色 *Bái sè*

Buy Sun

Yellow
黄色 *Huáng sè*

Juan Sun

SCIENCE AND TECHNOLOGY

Astronomy
天文学   *Tiān wén xué*

Tee Inn When Shoe

Calculator
计算器   *Jì suàn qì*

Jean Swan She

Chemistry
化学   *Huà xué*

Wash Eh

Computer
电脑   *Diàn nǎo*

Dee Ann Now

Computer memory
记忆体 *Jì yì tǐ*

Jean Eat Tee

Computer mouse
电脑鼠标
Diàn nǎo shǔ biāo

Dee Ann Now Sue Bee Out

Electricity
电力 *Diàn lì*

Dee Ann Lee

Illustration
插图 *Chā tú*

Chat Toe

Internet
因特网 *Yīn tè wǎng*

Inter Wong

Keyboard
键盘 *Jiàn pán*

Gin Pond

Laboratory
实验室 *Shí yàn shì*

She Ann She

Nuclear power
核电 *Hé diàn*

Hoodie End

Physics
物理　*Wù lǐ*

Who Lee

Rocket
火箭　*Huǒ jiàn*

Hoe Gin

Text
文本　*Wén běn*

1 Ben

Weapon
武器　*Wǔ qì*

Woo Cheap